THE CREDIT CHOICE
10 EFFECTIVE WAYS TO USE CREDIT CARDS WITHOUT GETTING INTO MAJOR DEBT

ROBERT F. NEWKIRK, JR.

© **Copyright 2024 - All rights reserved.**

The content contained within this book may not be reproduced, duplicated or transmitted without direct written permission from the author or the publisher.

Under no circumstances will any blame or legal responsibility be held against the publisher, or author, for any damages, reparation, or monetary loss due to the information contained within this book, either directly or indirectly.

Legal Notice:

This book is copyright protected. It is only for personal use. You cannot amend, distribute, sell, use, quote or paraphrase any part, or the content within this book, without the consent of the author or publisher.

Disclaimer Notice:

Please note the information contained within this document is for educational and entertainment purposes only. All effort has been executed to present accurate, up to date, reliable, complete information. No warranties of any kind are declared or implied. Readers acknowledge that the author is not engaged in the rendering of legal, financial, medical or professional advice. The content within this book has been derived from various sources. Please consult a licensed professional before attempting any techniques outlined in this book.

By reading this document, the reader agrees that under no circumstances is the author responsible for any losses, direct or indirect, that are incurred as a result of the use of the information contained within this document, including, but not limited to, errors, omissions, or inaccuracies.

CONTENTS

1. INTRODUCING THE CREDIT CHOICE	5
2. THE HIGH COST OF CREDIT CARDS	9
3. 10 EFFECTIVE WAYS TO USE CREDIT CARDS	11
1. Apply for Credit Cards With *No* Annual Fee	11
2. Use Rebate Credit Cards With the Lowest Interest Rates and Money Back Rewards	12
3. Use Personal Credit Cards as Cash	12
4. Use Credit Cards to Purchase Everyday Expenses	13
5. Pay Personal Credit Cards in *Full* Every Month	15
6. Reconcile Credit Cards Every Month	15
7. Manage All Recurring Expenses Placed on Credit Cards	19
8. Paying Late Fees and Other Miscellaneous Charges Are Nonnegotiable!	21
9. Carefully Plan When Using Credit Cards That Have "No Interest" Promotions	24
10. Plan Business Investment Using Credit Cards Such That Projected Profits Will Pay Off the Balance With as Little Interest as Possible	28
4. IMPLEMENTING THE CREDIT CHOICE	31

CHAPTER 1
INTRODUCING THE CREDIT CHOICE

Congratulations! We all have arrived, or are going to arrive, on the last day of our high school education. Some of us remember that day in our robes when we walked across the stage to receive our diplomas. Some of us may remember that day because we walked out of the school door for the last time, opting to pursue a vocation instead. Some may remember it by submitting the final test to qualify for a GED. Either way, school is over, so now what?

High school is the mark of becoming a grown-up and being on your own. That means it's time to make money! Unfortunately, the credit card companies know this and they are coming after you!

I remember my senior year in high school when I started accumulating a whole lot of mail from potential colleges that wanted me to apply to their school. However, as I approached graduation, the mail accumulation started shifting to more credit card applications: American Express, Visa Card, Mastercard, bank cards, airline cards, and so on. Each of them carried around $2,000 of credit, if I would only apply. There were so many choices and decisions I had to make at that time. Where will I live for the next four years? What did I want to study? What career did I want to pursue? What scholarships should I apply for? How much money did I need to secure in loans to make it through the first year? My thought process was stretched thin. Maybe I should go ahead and apply for a couple of these credit cards?

Unfortunately, our educational system has a history of not preparing us to responsibly answer these types of questions. Many people apply for these "free" credit cards with no credit history and see a piece of plastic that can easily buy things at the shopping mall. Have you ever wondered why the casinos in Las Vegas give you chips to put on the table as opposed to just using dollar bills? Subconsciously, people tend to forget that the red chips represent $20 and are more willing to throw chips on the table than the $20 itself. The same applies to plastic cards. I have a friend who went to college, got caught up in the credit card application frenzy, and found herself in an alarming amount of debt because she didn't realize that she had to pay the credit cards back after the purchases. She was not able to get out of credit card debt until she was 50 years old! So, everyone and college students, beware! You are the prey of credit card companies who would like you to be in debt to them for the next 30 years!

Financial stewardship is taking the position of a person who acts as a surrogate of others by managing financial affairs. This responsibility is necessary in order to oversee and protect something that is considered to be worth caring for and preserving. Society feeds off people who lack the qualities associated with financial stewardship, hoping that once they get their paycheck on Friday, they will have it all spent by Sunday. Money is a big "hot potato" that must immediately be taken out of your pocket and spent on things that have no real value. Credit cards only further fuel this frenzy. The first and foremost point is to avoid the trap of using newly acquired credit cards without realizing sooner or later that you will have to pay it back! Impulsive spending kills any chance of establishing long-term financial planning and is the antithesis of financial stewardship. Let's delve into the solution so that we do not become a victim and, ultimately, a financial slave to credit card companies.

Now, you may have already fallen victim to this situation. Maybe you have accumulated over $30,000 in credit card debt and have become paralyzed as to what the next steps are. If you find yourself in this situation, I recommend reading my book, *In-Debt to Debt-Free: Life's Roadmap to Financial Security*. It is a starting point on how to find your way out of debt and master money management so that you can take advantage of having *The Credit Choice*. As a lesson learned, whether the easy way or the hard way, credit cards must be used with discipline and purpose. If they are not used with discipline and purpose, impulsive and frivolous spending is the result.

I have heard a lot of financial advisors tell clients that the way to get out of credit card debt is to cut up their current credit cards or put them in the freezer, signifying that they are "freezing" their spending habits. Now, that may be sound advice for someone who has fallen victim to endless credit card debt, but that is also taking away a source of financial power that we have by having access to these credit cards. Credit cards can be used to build wealth and become financially free if they are used in their proper context. The proper context is what *The Credit Choice* is going to explain. *The Credit Choice* will help you learn how to leverage and manage your debt, teach you how to make money using credit cards, and, finally, explain 10 effective ways to use credit cards without getting into major debt.

Here, I need to explain that there are two different kinds of debt. First, there is bad debt, which the whole introduction has warned us to stay away from. Frivolous spending with credit cards and having no money in the bank to back it up certainly qualifies. Gambling away your rent money is also considered bad debt. We must take bad debt for what it is and learn how to manage it and move toward financial freedom. That leaves us with what is called good debt. This includes a mortgage that works toward gaining home ownership or a business loan that will help your business become profitable in the future. Using good debt will help us find our way to financial freedom faster. Let's explore why credit cards often create bad debt, how we can use credit cards as good debt, and what it takes to keep them as good debt.

CHAPTER 2
THE HIGH COST OF CREDIT CARDS

One of the things that I found separates the middle class from the wealthy is that the middle class believes in paying all their bills on time and working to become debt-free. This is a great philosophy to have; however, the caveat to having this philosophy is they do not like to borrow money even if it will benefit them financially in the long term, whereas the wealthy believe in using other people's money to start new initiatives versus using their own money. It gives them the power of choice that helps them achieve their goals while keeping their own money—they become masters at managing other people's money.

I can understand this difference from both sides, particularly with the high cost of borrowing money using credit cards. The average interest rate for credit cards rose to 24.4% versus 18% in 1995. In addition, the minimum payment percentage each month on credit cards averages 10.2% compared to 4% in 1995. The problem with these conditions is that if we spend $1,100 on credit cards and only pay the minimum payment every month, it will take over 20 years to pay off that $1,100 principal in full! Once we finally pay off that

$1,100 principal, we will have accrued and paid over $2,700 in interest by the time it is paid in full. The original $1,100 principal ends up becoming $3,800 when it's finally paid in full! In other words, over 70% of the total to pay off $1,100 went to interest, not principal.

I know because I was brought up with this position toward money. Life's uncontrollable nature has taught me that I must get over this if I am going to achieve success. Think of it this way: Not too long ago, the price of eggs jumped from $1.59 per dozen to $5.99 per dozen! Everybody was very upset that they had to pay $5.99 to make an omelet at home. If they get upset that easily over paying $5.99 for a carton of eggs, why are they not beside themselves when they use $1,100 in credit, with no means but to pay it off with minimum payments, and ultimately end up paying $3,800 for $1,100 worth of merchandise? The percentages are the same.

It makes sense for the middle class to be skeptical about obtaining debt. That perspective comes because the middle class is looking for comfort. There is a comfort associated with being debt-free. However, the wealthy are not looking for comfort. They are looking for achievement, freedom, and success. They will use every resource available to them to get it. They are constantly borrowing to make a return on their investment with other people's money. Mastering money management is the key. The challenge is you must choose where you want to end up in this category. If it is comfort that you seek, the middle class is waiting for you. If you want achievement, freedom, and success, a new framework must be created and you must master managing money, including your credit cards.

CHAPTER 3
10 EFFECTIVE WAYS TO USE CREDIT CARDS

If we desire to use our credit cards efficiently and effectively, we must understand the power that credit cards possess and the ways we can use them to accomplish our achievements, freedom, and success. I have come up with 10 effective ways to use your credit cards without recreating the previous example above and paying over three times the amount you borrowed. Let's get into these effective strategies.

1. APPLY FOR CREDIT CARDS WITH *NO* ANNUAL FEE

I do not believe in donating to charities with no cause. Paying an annual fee to hold someone's credit card, in my opinion, fits that category. I have seen companies that charge up to $99 per year to hold their card and upward of $599 per year to hold a gold or platinum card, and they don't allow you to keep a balance from month to month. I can think of a million things that I can do every year using that $99. Plus, there are plenty of credit cards, both personal and business, that do not have an annual fee associated with them. As soon as I see that an application mentions an annual fee, I tear it into pieces.

2. USE REBATE CREDIT CARDS WITH THE LOWEST INTEREST RATES AND MONEY BACK REWARDS

The use of rebate credit cards is a great setup to help us make money for which we never have to lift a finger. Since the credit card industry has become so competitive within its own ranks, several credit cards offer a 1%, 2%, or even, in some cases, 3% rebate on different categories of purchases made with the card. That gives us a lot of leverage on how we structure spending habits and methods of paying for everyday expenses. Where the credit companies get us is when we do not pay our balance on time. If we do not regularly pay our balance in full and on time every month, the amount we receive on rebates will be canceled by accruing interest, late fees, and other "soft fees" justified by late payments. It is imperative that we actively manage our credit cards in order to maximize the rebates we receive.

3. USE PERSONAL CREDIT CARDS AS CASH

I must say it again: Impulsive spending kills long-term financial planning. It also kills any chance of building wealth and retirement. To counter the use of credit cards for impulsive spending, we must view personal credit cards as substitutes for cash that we currently have or will soon have in the bank. Never view personal credit cards as credit or as an advance for money that has not yet been earned or given. This must be done with discipline and a purpose. How do we determine if there is cash in the bank for the purchase we are about to make? This is where budgeting and accounting come into play. It is bad practice to look solely at your current balance in your bank account to determine whether you have cash on hand to make a transaction. Most impulsive spenders use this method to make their last-minute purchases. The problem is that most of the time, the money currently in the bank was already allocated for a previous purchase that was made and, therefore, cannot account for your current purchase. Finding ourselves adhering to this method of accountability is truly using credit cards as credit!

4. USE CREDIT CARDS TO PURCHASE EVERYDAY EXPENSES

The perfect opportunity to implement Steps 2 and 3 is to implement Step 4: Instead of using cash, keep the cash in the bank and use the credit card to make everyday purchases in accordance with your monthly budget. This includes groceries, gas, mailing services, eating out, grabbing fast food, and other retail expenditures. When I say "expenditures," I am speaking of what is necessary for everyday living, such as providing food, clothing, and shelter. We can also use our credit cards to pay for our phone services, electricity, travel expenses, gym memberships, and so on. The method behind the madness is that if we use a credit card to pay for expenses, we can hold on to the money used for, at a minimum, 30 additional days while the credit card company processes the payment and organizes the billing invoice that is sent at the end of the billing period. Once it is received, we have anywhere from 20–30 days before the bill is due. In the meantime, we can keep the cash for up to an additional 30–60 days in an investment or money market account, accruing interest during that period. In addition, by using a credit card with cash-back rewards, we are constantly accumulating the rebate associated with the card with purchases that we would have to pay for anyway. Below is a copy of a bank statement from a

14 THE CREDIT CHOICE

few years back that shows the cash rewards of the 1% rebate I earned for that period and the reward dollars that had accumulated and were available for my use.

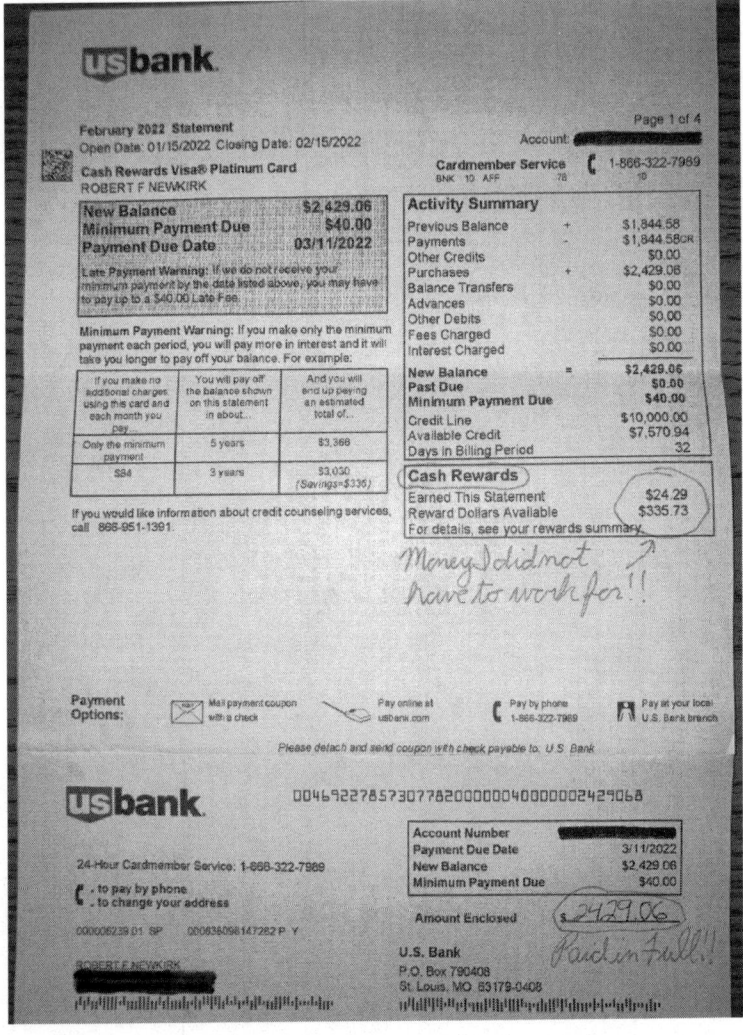

5. PAY PERSONAL CREDIT CARDS IN *FULL* EVERY MONTH

In the USBank statement above, notice in the lower right-hand corner that the amount due for that month was paid in full! It is imperative that all personal credit cards are paid in full each cycle. If not, then we are negating the gains achieved by applying Steps 1–4. When you are paying your bills, make sure that all the items listed on your bill are legitimate items you purchased the previous month. Every time I receive my billing statement, I always look at the activity summary, as shown in the upper right-hand corner of the previously shown statement. It should verify what the previous balance was, what payment credits were applied to the statement, and any other credits that were applied during the payment cycle. The inputs that I am most concerned about are the fees charged and the interest charged. If those charges are anything other than zero, I will immediately call the card member service number listed above the activity summary and inquire as to why those charges are being administered. This is the luxury we have when we pay the balance in full every month. We now have the leverage with the credit card company in lowering interest rates and challenging charges that should not be there.

6. RECONCILE CREDIT CARDS EVERY MONTH

Of the ten ways in which to effectively use credit cards, this is by far the most important step to execute on a habitual basis. The main reason that we must reconcile our credit cards is we must ensure that there are no unwarranted charges included on our statement, ultimately leading to your credit payments. Many people fail to even look at their statements, let alone

16 THE CREDIT CHOICE

reconcile them. Missing one statement can cause you to pay off an interest-bearing charge that was not even made. Look at the Discover credit statement below.

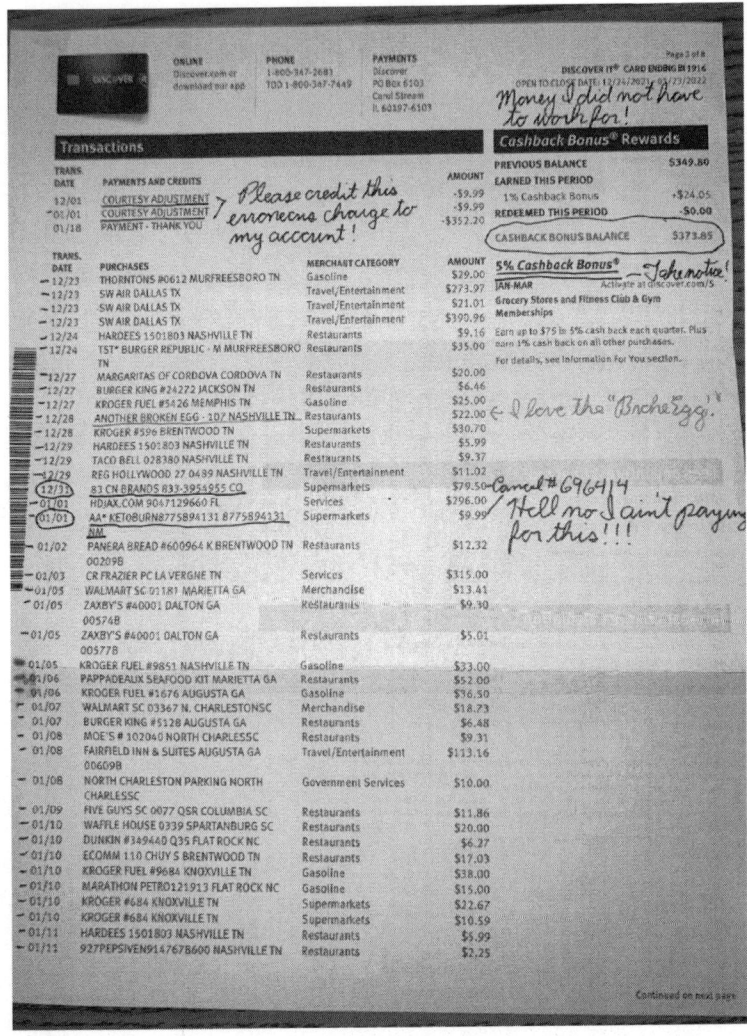

By the way, remember what was said in Step 2? Look at the upper right-hand corner of the statement where it says, "Cashback Bonus Rewards." Look at what I have circled: "Cashback Bonus Balance: $373.85"! That is the amount I had accumulated by purchasing everyday expenses on that card since my anniversary date in June. Also, notice the line titled "Earned This Period," with my 1% cashback bonus, I earned $24.05! The categories that I used this card for during this statement period were gasoline, travel, restaurants, supermarkets, services, and merchandise. All everyday expenses: Money I was required to spend in order to live through the course of the month. Rebate cards are a great way to make money you do not have to work for!

The statement page above is filled with comments I made regarding the importance of reconciling your statements. There is one transaction that is underlined, dated 01/01, from AA*KETOBURN with a phone number beside it. Apparently, the company is out of New Mexico, and they charged me $9.99 for something I have no clue about. Well, you might say that is not a big deal; it is only $9.99. Wrong! It is a *big* deal! First, it is $10! They use the gimmick of saying it is $9.99 because it sounds less than $10, and they are hoping that you will see it as no big deal. Second, if we reconcile this correctly, we will discover this is a recurring charge! Not only did I not make this charge with my credit card, but they have also been repeatedly charging me $9.99, hoping I would miss it and let the charge slide through.

How did they get my credit card number in the first place? I didn't give it to them. Notice my comment to the side of the charge that says, "Hell no, I ain't paying for this!!!" with the cancellation number on top of it. Yes, upon discovering this erroneous charge, I immediately called Discover card member services to address the issue. If you look above at the top of the "transactions" section, you will notice that this recurring charge was not noticed by me the first time I looked at this statement. At the beginning of December and the beginning of January, I had already requested an adjustment to the same charge by the same company I did not purchase from. They labeled it as a "courtesy adjustment." Then they filled out a fraudulent report regarding the erroneous charge incident, closed that credit card number, and issued me a new card number, sending the card in the mail. You will see my notation on the statement, "Please credit this erroneous charge to my account!"

Now, what would have happened in this situation if I had not been reconciling my credit card account during this period? This recurring charge would have folded into the overall balance, and by the month of March, I would have had no idea what I was paying for when finally submitting a payment to them. That simple, no-big-deal $9.99 charge would suddenly be a whopping $39.96! *I don't think so.* I will say it again: Reconcile your credit card statements *every* month!

7. MANAGE ALL RECURRING EXPENSES PLACED ON CREDIT CARDS

Do I need to reiterate the incident that occurred while explaining Step 6? Absolutely not. However, there is another angle to this step that also needs to be addressed. What about the charges that we *do* authorize to be charged to our credit card? Okay, let's go back to the charge of $9.99. No big deal, right? As an example, let's use the fact that I have an iPhone and along with that comes Apple Music. I have my old music, which I purchased from iTunes a while back for $0.99 per song. Now, they will allow me access to any song off any album I choose. The only caveat is that I have to pay them $9.99+ tax for the access. Well, I have succumbed to that charge because if I decided to cancel my service with Apple Music, all the playlists of different genres of music that I have made over the years would be deactivated, leaving me with only the songs I received through a singular purchase. Oh, well, for that one. Now, what would happen if I decided to watch Netflix on my television? That costs $15.49 per month, another recurring charge! Wait, I have to purchase Disney+ so that I can watch all the Marvel movies and the Pirates of the Caribbean series! How much will that cost? That will be $13.99 per month coming out of my pocket. This is the point I am making. Look at the list in the picture below:

20 THE CREDIT CHOICE

Now, the prices here are from before all the streaming networks started raising their prices recently, but you get the idea. The whole list here sums up to $139.87 per month! That comes out to a whopping $1,678.44 per year! That is a lot of money to be sucked up due to recurring costs. Yet, a lot of people have subscriptions to every one of them, but they do not realize the total amount of money swallowed up by having access to these channels and services. We all need to evaluate the necessity of having access and determine whether it is worth keeping all of them. If there are ones that are not living up to their recurring value, be sure to cancel them.

8. PAYING LATE FEES AND OTHER MISCELLANEOUS CHARGES ARE NONNEGOTIABLE!

Let me be clear: I refuse to pay for any late fees or other miscellaneous charges that may appear on my credit card statements. In my opinion, paying late charges is the dumbest way to lose your money! What are you getting for paying a late fee? That goes for any other fee that you might have to pay. If it is necessary to pay a fee, then there is something that you should be gaining from paying that fee. I have a mindset that I instilled in my children: If you are preparing to take a test or a certification that you must pay a fee to take, you should know without a doubt that you are going to pass that test and receive that certification once you are finished with the process. It should only be a matter of procedure for you to get that certification. If you are not sure beyond a shadow of a doubt that you will get it once you take the test, wait until you are sure. Never go into a test uncertain whether you will pass. To me, that's another way of donating to a charity with no cause. The same goes for paying fees to credit card companies. You are donating money to the credit card company for no reason whatsoever. Commit to not paying it, which means doing the planning necessary to ensure you are not paying late fees.

There is one power that we have when we continually execute Steps 1–7. When we have control over our spending habits and we pay our credit card statements on time, we increase our credit scores, and the credit card companies appreciate having us as customers. Therefore, when we call in about a discrepancy of some kind, they take heed to make sure that we are happy once the call is over and we continue to be their

22 THE CREDIT CHOICE

customers. This is why I can take the pledge that late fees and miscellaneous charges are nonnegotiable for me. I refuse to pay them even if I am the cause of the charges! Look at the first page of my Discover card statement:

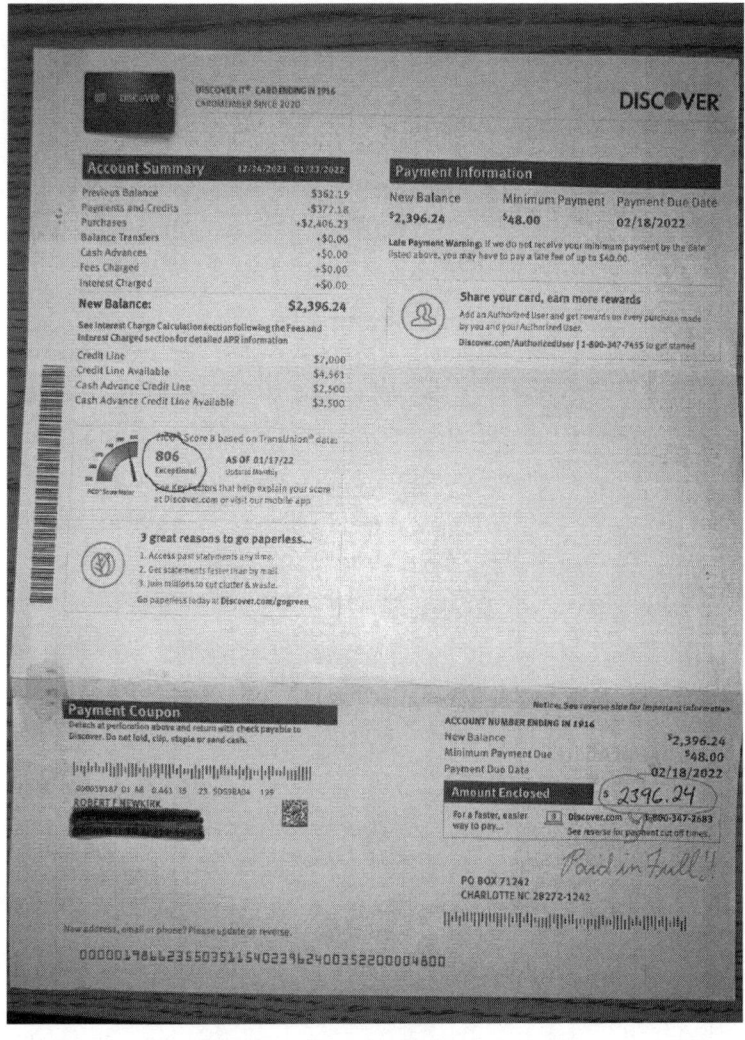

If you look at the middle of the page to the left, it shows what my FICO score is based on TransUnion data. My score is 806 at this point, which is classified as an exceptional score. Also, note on that page that the amount of the credit card statement was paid in full!

FICO is simply a company (Fair Isaac Corporation), founded in the late 1950s in Bozeman, Montana, that established a credit scoring system that serves as a measure of consumer credit risk for consumer lenders. Credit lenders need a fast and consistent way to determine whether giving a loan to someone is high risk. The factors of a FICO score measure how long you have had credit, how much credit you have, how much of your credit is currently being used, and if you have a history of paying on time. A high FICO score gives you leverage with credit card companies. As an example, I went to a hamburger place while I was in Florida and ordered a combo with my favorite burger. The total was supposed to be $11.43. Somehow, the cashier rang up two combo orders and charged me $22.89. I caught it immediately, and he adjusted the charge to $11.43. When I received my statement, I saw that the charge for the burger was still showing as $22.89. So, I called card member services and told them the charge was $11.43 instead of $22.89. What the card member representative did surprised me; they gave me a courtesy credit for the entire $22.89! It was a credit for my inconvenience! Okay, I will accept that. However, I am certain that if my FICO score was labeled as fair or poor, I would not have gotten that courtesy offer.

Here is another example I would like to share with you: One month, I was reconciling my credit card statement, and I wrote a check for the full amount to mail to the credit card company (yes, this example happened over 25 years ago when people still mailed checks in). The next month's bill came along, and I noticed that the statement had a late fee listed and an interest charge attached to it. I was baffled by the situation because I was sure I had written a check for the full amount. I checked my accounting ledger, and sure enough, it had listed that the full amount had been paid. I looked through the envelope that contained all of my bills for the month. To my surprise, within the bill's envelope lay the credit card mailer with the check inside. I had failed to put the check in the mail. Well, there was no time like the present to go out to the mailbox and stick the bill in. Then I came back to my desk and called cardmember services. I made mention of the late fee and the interest charge, and they responded that they had not received my payment from the previous month. I told them that I had written a check for the full amount and that it was in the mail! I said that if they did not receive the check within the next couple of days, I would write another check for the full amount and send it to them. However, I needed them to credit the late fee and the interest charge back to my account. Now, I can't remember whether I had to talk to a supervisor or not, but nevertheless, in the end, they did credit both the late fee and the interest charge back to my account. That's what I mean by nonnegotiable!

9. CAREFULLY PLAN WHEN USING CREDIT CARDS THAT HAVE "NO INTEREST" PROMOTIONS

Credit card companies love to use the "No Interest for a Year" gimmick to lure newcomers to sign up for their credit card and immediately start charging things to their accounts. "I can purchase this new furniture and not have to make any payments on it for 24 months! Yahoo!" This is the thinking of a lot of people who initially signed up for this type of promotion.

However, this statement is far from the truth. Let me explain. No interest is a golden nugget that credit card companies use to get you to sign up. It is true no interest will be charged to you for a year or however long the terms of the agreement call for. I have seen the terms for as long as three years. However, that does not mean interest is not accruing on the account. Up to 28% could be accrued onto the account; however, it will not be added to the account total until the deadline of the terms of the agreement is up.

In other words, if I open the account in August of year 1, the terms of the agreement might list the deadline of terms date as July 31 of year 2. If I do not pay the card in full by the July date, not only will I be charged interest for the month of July, but I will also be charged the total accrued interest from when I first opened the card. Do not fall victim to this gimmick. If we decide to use the new credit card to delay payments for a period, be sure to have a plan to pay in full when the period is up.

Another issue to be aware of is that the term "no interest" does not mean that no payment is due until the period is up. The credit card company will charge you what is considered the minimum payment each month throughout the "no interest" period.

26 THE CREDIT CHOICE

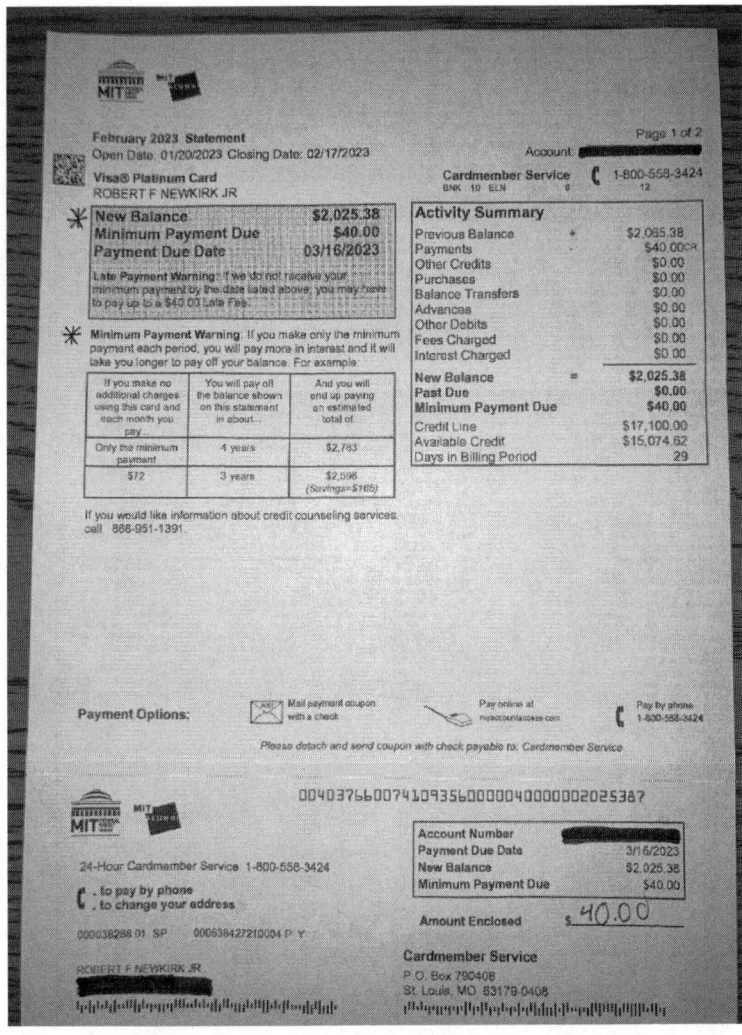

Refer to the block where it says "New Balance" in the statement above. Credit card companies are required to include a "late payment warning" and a minimum payment warning on the card statements. The late payment warning usually says if the company does not receive your minimum payment by the date listed, you may have to pay up to a certain amount, which is considered the "late fee." By not paying the minimum payment by the monthly due date, late charges will be added to the account, which I have already mentioned is a nonnegotiable charge. In addition, the "minimum payment warning" reminds you that if you make only the minimum payment each period, you will pay more in interest and it will take longer to pay off the balance. Now, look at the statement below.

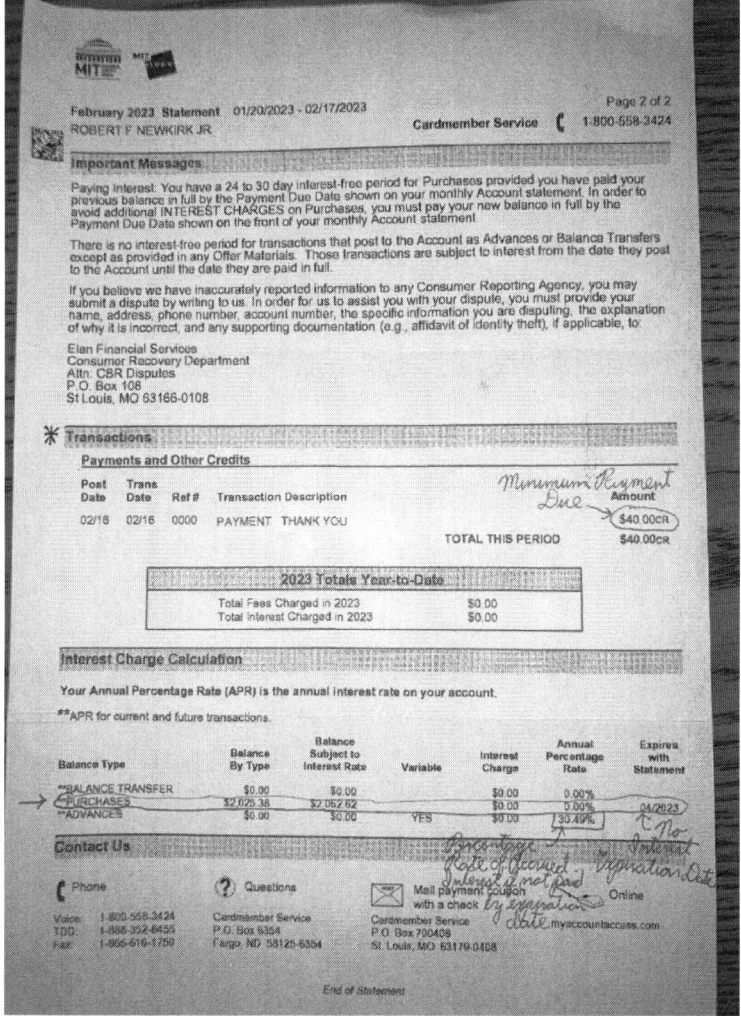

Look at the middle section titled "Transactions." This is a card that I signed up for that had no interest for 15 months. Notice that I still had to make a payment each month that was equivalent to the minimum payment due. Looking below is a section titled "Interest Charge Calculation." Here, it shows that I have a purchase balance of $2,062.62 that is subject to the interest rate in the terms of the agreement, which was 24.99%. To the right of that circled line, it shows an "Expires with Statement" date of 04/2023. That means I must pay off the balance of $2,062.62 by the last statement due date before the month ends. Otherwise, the total amount of accrued interest from the time I first opened the card will be charged. You best believe that I paid that card off in full by the expiration date!

10. PLAN BUSINESS INVESTMENT USING CREDIT CARDS SUCH THAT PROJECTED PROFITS WILL PAY OFF THE BALANCE WITH AS LITTLE INTEREST AS POSSIBLE

The preceding 9 steps were dealing with personal credit cards. Step 10 only applies when you are looking to start a business or become an entrepreneur. First, credit cards, if possible, should be the last resort for businesses to obtain capital, as credit cards usually come with the highest interest rates of all loaning opportunities. It is more affordable to get a loan from a bank, a financial lender, or an angel investor. However, these types of loans are often hard to come by, particularly for a brand-new business that has not yet built a reputation. In this case, credit cards may become the most viable option.

Cash flow is king for any business to function. If using credit cards is necessary, then as the decision maker of the business, you have to ensure infusing capital from credit cards will generate the profits necessary to pay off the credit card balance in the shortest period possible. If not, then the high interest rates associated with credit cards will continue to accrue, building more debt that the business must recover from in order to have a chance at becoming profitable. The plan should be to have the credit cards paid in full within six months at most of first using them.

Business credit cards have become an option over the years to keep business owner's personal credit scores separate from their business credit. Ironically, it is usually the business owner's personal credit score that allows them to get business credit. However, these types of credit cards are often the ones most available to newly established businesses. The warning once again is not to become the credit customer who is so indebted to their credit provider that the only solution for the business is bankruptcy. Credit card ownership brings an insurmountable amount of high risk with it and the possibility of taking on unnecessary liability.

CHAPTER 4
IMPLEMENTING THE CREDIT CHOICE

The Credit Choice is a decision maker. If we find ourselves at a point of plateau in our business, our finances, and our relationships where our valley seems to be taking over our transitions in life, *The Credit Choice* is designed to bring focus, motivation, and purpose to our new creation. Creation is the beginning of a new unknown, the birth of what has never been before. *The Credit Choice* facilitates the start of resource channeling to fuel "the what" being created. John H. Johnson, the founder and chief executive of Ebony magazine, once said, "Money is the greatest measurement of your mindset. Wealth is less a matter of circumstance than it is a matter of knowledge and choice. You must take control of your life—you must make the decision to be wealthy." This philosophy must trickle down if we are to be successful using credit cards in our journey to achieve success. Therefore, it is imperative that we understand all the pros and cons of using credit cards and take advantage of them. If we are effective in using credit cards, we allow ourselves the opportunity to become financially free much faster. *The Credit Choice* helps us maintain discipline and create purpose in using credit cards that will help us make money in the long run as opposed to obtaining major debt.

I am thrilled that you took the time to read and comprehend *The Credit Choice*. Only 16.4% of U.S. students are required to take a personal finance class in schools, and four out of five adults say they were never given the opportunity to learn about personal finance. The problem most people face is not having enough money but frustration because they feel they are doing everything they can, but no progress is being made in paying down credit cards. They are afraid of not having enough money for college and retirement or being able to manage their income well enough to make ends meet. My intent for *The Credit Choice* is to put you on the runway heading toward freedom amid financial confusion. As far as gaining discipline in your finances, you can now make the pilgrimage that will allow you to earn more, save more, serve more, create more, and spend a whole lot less.

Made in the USA
Columbia, SC
07 December 2024